The Keepsake Book of
Christmas Carols

The Keepsake Book of

CHRISTMAS CAROLS

Running Press

Philadelphia, Pennsylvania

9 8 7 6 5 4 3 2 1
Digit on the right indicates the number of this printing.

Library of Congress Card Catalog Number: 84–758183

ISBN: 0–89471–281–0 (paper)

Researched and newly edited by Tam Mossman.
Designed by Madge Schultz.
Cover design by Toby Schmidt.
Illustrated by Geri Greinke.
Typography: Weiss, by rci, Philadelphia, Pennsylvania.
Printed by Howard Printing, Huntingdon Valley, Pennsylvania.

This book can be ordered by mail
from the publisher. Please include $1.00 for postage.
But try your bookstore first.
Running Press
Book Publishers
125 South 22nd Street
Philadelphia, Pennsylvania 19103

♣ C O N T E N T S ♣

(In alphabetical order)

Angels We Have Heard on High 8

Away in a Manger 10

Christmas is Coming 13

Deck the Halls 14

The First Noel 19

God Rest Ye Merry, Gentlemen 16

Good King Wenceslas 22

Hark! The Herald Angels Sing 26

It Came Upon the Midnight Clear 24

Jingle, Bells 28

Jolly Old Saint Nicholas 34

Joy to the World 37

Oh Christmas Tree 32

Oh Come, All Ye Faithful 38

Oh Holy Night! 35

Oh Little Town of Bethlehem 42

Silent Night 48

The Twelve Days of Christmas 30

Up on the Rooftop 44

We Three Kings of Orient Are 11

We Wish You a Merry Christmas 40

What Child is This? 46

Angels We Have Heard on High

Angels we have heard on high,
  Sweetly singing o'er the plains;
And the mountains, in reply,
  Echoing their joyous strains:

CHORUS:
  Gloria in excelsis Deo,
  Gloria in excelsis Deo!

Shepherds, why this jubilee?
  Why your joyful strains prolong?
What the gladsome tidings be
  That inspire your heav'nly song?

CHORUS

Come to Bethlehem and see
  Him whose birth the angels sing.
Come adore on bended knee
  Christ the Lord, our newborn King.

CHORUS

See Him in a manger laid,
  Whom the choirs of angels praise.
Mary, Joseph, lend your aid
  While our hearts in love we raise.

CHORUS

AWAY IN A MANGER

Away in a manger, no crib for a bed,
The little Lord Jesus laid down His sweet head.
The stars in the heavens looked down where He lay:
The little Lord Jesus, asleep in the hay.

The cattle are lowing. The baby awakes,
But little Lord Jesus, no crying He makes.
I love Thee, Lord Jesus! Look down from the sky,
And stay by my cradle till morning is nigh.

Be near me, Lord Jesus! I ask Thee to stay
Close by me forever and love me, I pray.
Bless all the dear children in Thy tender care,
And take us to heaven to live with Thee there.

WE THREE KINGS OF ORIENT ARE

We three kings of Orient are.
Bearing gifts, we traverse afar—
Field and fountain, moor and mountain—
   Following yonder star.

CHORUS:

Oh, star of wonder, star of night,
Star of royal beauty bright,
Westward leading, still proceeding,
Guide us to thy perfect light.

[MELCHIOR:]
Born a king on Bethlehem's plain—
   Gold I bring, to crown Him again—
King for ever, ceasing never,
   Over us all to reign.

CHORUS

[GASPAR:]
Frankincense to offer have I.
   Incense owns a Deity nigh.
Prayer and praising, all men raising,
   Worship Him, God most high!

CHORUS

[continued]

[BALTHAZAR:]

Myrrh is mine: its bitter perfume
　　Breathes a life of gathering gloom,
Sorrowing, sighing, bleeding, dying,
　　Sealed in the stone-cold tomb.

CHORUS

[ALL:]

Glorious now, behold Him arise:
　　King and God and sacrifice!
Heav'n sings, "*Ha*-le-lu-ia!" "*Ha*-ah-le-
　　Lu-ia!" the Earth replies.

CHORUS

CHRISTMAS IS COMING

*C*hristmas is coming.
The geese are getting fat.
Please to put a penny
   In the old man's hat.
If you haven't got a penny,
   A ha'penny'll do.
If you haven't got a ha'penny,
   God bless you!

Deck the Halls

Deck the halls with boughs of holly.
   Fa la la la la, la la la la.
'Tis the season to be jolly.
   Fa la la la la, la la la la.
Don we now our gay apparel.
   Fa la la, la la la, la la la.
Troll the ancient Yuletide carol:
   Fa la la la la, la la la la.

See the blazing Yule before us.
   Fa la la la la, la la la la.
Strike the harp and join the chorus.
   Fa la la la la, la la la la.
Follow me in merry measure—
   Fa la la, la la la, la la la—
While I tell of Yuletide treasure.
   Fa la la la la, la la la la.

Fast away the old year passes.
   Fa la la la la, la la la la.
Hail the new, ye lads and lasses.
   Fa la la la la, la la la la.
Sing we joyous, all together—
   Fa la la, la la la, la la la—
Heedless of the wind and weather.
   Fa la la la la, la la la la.

GOD REST YE MERRY, GENTLEMEN

God rest ye merry, gentlemen;
Let nothing you dismay.
Remember, Christ our Savior
    Was born on Christmas Day,
To save us all from Satan's pow'r
    When we had gone astray.

CHORUS:
    Oh, tidings of comfort and joy,
    Comfort and joy,
    Oh, tidings of comfort and joy!

'Twas in the town of Bethlehem
    This blessed Babe was born.
They laid Him in a manger
    Where oxen feed on corn,
And Mary knelt and prayed to God
    Upon that blessed morn.

CHORUS

From God our Heav'nly Father
    A host of angels came
Unto some certain shepherds
    With tidings of the same:
That there was born in Bethlehem
    The Son of God by name.

CHORUS

"Fear not," then said the angels,
   "Let nothing you affright.
This day is born a Savior
   Of virtue, pow'r, and might—
To ransom you from Sin and Death
   And vanquish Satan quite."

CHORUS

The shepherds, at these tidings,
   Rejoicèd much in mind,
And on that windy plain they left
   Their sleeping flocks behind,
And straight they went to Bethlehem,
   Their newborn King to find.

CHORUS

Now when they came to Bethlehem,
   Where our sweet Savior lay,
They found Him in a manger,
   Where oxen feed on hay.
His blessed Mother, kneeling down,
   Unto the Lord did pray.

CHORUS

With sudden joy and gladness
   The shepherds were beguiled,
To see the King of Israel
   And Holy Mary mild.
With them, in cheerfulness and love
   Rejoice each mother's child!

[continued]

17

CHORUS

Now to the Lord sing praises,
  All you within this place,
And in true loving brotherhood
  Each other now embrace,
For Christmas doth in all inspire
  A glad and cheerful face.

CHORUS

God bless the master of this house
  And grant him long to reign,
That many merry Christmas Eves
  May come his way again;
God bless your friends and kindred folk
  Who live both far and near,
And God send you a happy New Year!

THE FIRST NOEL

The first Noel the angels did say
Was to certain poor shepherds in fields as they lay—
In fields where they lay, keeping their sheep,
  On a cold winter's night that was so deep.

  CHORUS:
  Noel, Noel, Noel, Noel,
  Born is the King of Israel!

They lookèd up and saw a star,
  Shining in the East, but beyond them far.
And unto the Earth it gave great light,
  And so it continued, both day and night.

  CHORUS

And by the light of that same star
  Three Wise Men came from country far.
To seek for a King was their intent,
  And to follow the star wherever it went.

  CHORUS

This star drew nigh to the northwest.
  Over Bethlehem it took its rest,
And there it did both stop and stay
  Right over the stable where Jesus lay.

  CHORUS

[continued]

Then they did know and in wonder confide
   That within that house a King did reside.
One entered in then, with his own eyes to see
   And discovered the Babe in poverty.

Chorus

Between the stalls of the oxen, forlorn,
   This Child on that cold night in truth was born.
And for want of a crib, Mary did Him lay
   In the depths of a manger amongst the hay.

Chorus

Then entered in all those Wise Men three,
   Fell reverently upon bended knee,
And offered there, in His presence,
   Gifts of gold and of myrrh and of frankincense.

Chorus

So let us all, with one single accord,
   Sing glad praises unto our Heavenly Lord,
Who hath fashioned the Earth and heavens of naught,
   And with His blood mankind hath bought.

Chorus

And if we in our time shall live upright and well,
   We shall be set free from death and from Hell,
For God hath prepared for us all
   A resting place in general.

Chorus

GOOD KING WENCESLAS

ood King Wenceslas looked out
On the Feast of Stephen,
When the snow lay 'round about,
Deep and crisp and even.
Brightly shone the moon that night,
Though the frost was cruel,
When a poor man came in sight,
Gath'ring winter fuël.

"Hither, page, and stand by me!
If thou hast heard telling,
Yonder peasant—who is he?
Where and what his dwelling?"
"Sire, he lives a good league hence,
Underneath the mountain,
Right against the forest fence
By Saint Agnes' fountain."

"Bring me flesh and bring me wine!
Bring me pine-logs hither!
Thou and I will see him dine
When we bear them thither."
Page and monarch, forth they went;
Forth they went together,
Through the rude wind's wild lament
And the bitter weather.

"Sire, the night grows darker now,
    And the wind blows stronger.
Fails my heart—I know not how
    I can go much longer!"
"Mark my footsteps, my good page.
    Tread thou in them boldly.
Thou shall feel this winter's rage
    Freeze thy blood less coldly."

In his master's steps he trod,
    Where the snow lay dinted.
Heat was in the very sod
    Which the Saint had printed.
Therefore, Christian men, be sure,
    Wealth or rank possessing,
Ye who now will bless the poor
    Shall yourselves find blessing.

It Came Upon the Midnight Clear

It came upon the midnight clear,
   That glorious song of old,
From angels bending near the Earth
   To touch their harps of gold:
"Peace on the Earth! Good will to men,
   From Heaven's all-gracious King!"
The world in solemn stillness lay
   To hear the angels sing.

Still through the cloven skies they come,
   With seraphs' wings unfurled;
And still their heavenly music floats
   O'er all the weary world.
Above its sad and lowly plains
   They bend on hovering wing.
And ever o'er its Babel sounds
   The blessed angels sing.

Yet with the woes of sin and strife,
   The world has suffered long.
Beneath the angels' strains have rolled
   Two thousand years of wrong;
And man, at war with man, hears not
   The love-song which they bring.
Oh, hush the noise, ye men of strife,
   And hear the angels sing!

And ye, beneath life's crushing load,
  Whose shoulders are bending low,
Who toil along the climbing way
  With painful steps and slow—
Take heart! For comfort, hope, and joy
  Come swiftly on the wing.
Oh, rest beside the weary road
  And hear the angels sing!

For lo! The days are hast'ning on,
  As prophets knew of old,
And with the ever-circling years
  Comes 'round the time foretold,
When love shall reign, and men declare
  The Prince of Peace their King;
And all the Earth send back the song
  Which now the angels sing.

Hark! The Herald Angels Sing

ark! The herald angels sing,
   "Glory to the newborn King!
Peace on Earth and mercy mild,
   God and sinners reconciled."
Joyful all ye nations, rise!
   Join the triumph of the skies.
With th'angelic host, proclaim,
   "Christ is born in Bethlehem!"

CHORUS:
   Hark! The herald angels sing,
   "Glory to the newborn King!"

Christ, by highest Heav'n adored;
   Christ, the everlasting Lord:
Late in time, behold Him come,
   Offspring of the Virgin's womb.
Veiled in flesh the Godhead see.
   Hail th'Incarnate Deity
Pleased as Man with men to dwell—
   Jesus, our Emmanuel!

CHORUS

Mild He lays His glory by,
   Born that man no more may die,
Born to raise the sons of Earth,
   Born to give them second birth.

Light and life to all He brings,
    Ris'n with healing in His wings.
Hail, the Sun of Righteousness!
    Hail, the Heav'n-born Prince of Peace!

CHORUS

27

JINGLE, BELLS

Dashing through the snow
  In a one-horse open sleigh,
O'er the field we go,
  Laughing all the way.
Bells on bobtail ring,
  Making spirits bright.
What fun it is to laugh and sing
  A sleighing song tonight!

CHORUS:
  Jingle, bells! Jingle, bells!
  Jingle all the way!
  Oh, what fun it is to ride
  In a one-horse open sleigh—hey!
  Jingle, bells! Jingle, bells!
  Jingle all the way!
  Oh, what fun it is to ride
  In a one-horse open sleigh!

A day or two ago,
  I thought I'd take a ride,
And soon Miss Fannie Bright
  Was seated by my side.
The horse was lean and lank,
  But hardly worth his hay.
He veered into a drifted bank
  And overturned the sleigh!

CHORUS

Now the ground is white.
    Go for it while you're young.
Take the girls tonight
    And sing this sleighing song.
Just rent a bobtail'd bay,
    Two-forty for his speed.
Then hitch him to an open sleigh,
    And crack! you'll take the lead!

CHORUS

You won't mind the cold,
    The robe is thick and warm.
Snow falls on the road,
    Silv'ring every form.
The woods are dark and still.
    The horse is trotting fast.
He'll pull the sleigh around the hill
    And home again at last.

CHORUS

THE TWELVE DAYS OF CHRISTMAS

On the first day of Christmas,
My true love gave to me
A partridge in a pear tree.

On the second day of Christmas,
   My true love gave to me
Two turtle doves, and a partridge in a pear tree.

On the third day of Christmas,
   My true love gave to me
Three French hens,
Two turtle doves, and a partridge in a pear tree.

On the fourth day of Christmas . . .
Four calling birds, . . .

On the fifth day of Christmas . . .
Five golden rings; . . .

On the sixth day of Christmas . . .
Six geese a-laying, . . .

On the seventh day of Christmas . . .
Seven swans a-swimming, . . .

On the eighth day of Christmas . . .
Eight maids a-milking, . . .

On the ninth day of Christmas . . .
Nine ladies dancing, . . .

On the tenth day of Christmas . . .
Ten lords a-leaping, . . .

On the eleventh day of Christmas . . .
Eleven pipers piping, . . .

On the twelfth day of Christmas,
   My true love gave to me
Twelve drummers drumming,
Eleven pipers piping,
Ten lords a-leaping,
Nine ladies dancing,
Eight maids a-milking,
Seven swans a-swimming,
Six geese a-laying,
Five golden rings;
Four calling birds,
Three French hens,
Two turtle doves,
And a partridge in a pear tree.

OH CHRISTMAS TREE
[O Tannenbaum]

O h Christmas Tree, Oh Christmas Tree,
  With lush green boughs unchanging—
Green when the summer sun is bright,
  And when the forest's cold and white.
Oh Christmas Tree, Oh Christmas Tree,
  With lush green boughs unchanging!

Oh Christmas Tree, Oh Christmas Tree,
  Here once again to awe us,
You bear round fruits of Christmas past,
  Spun out of silver, gold, and glass.
Oh Christmas Tree, Oh Christmas Tree,
  Here once again to awe us!

Oh Christmas Tree, Oh Christmas Tree,
  We gladly bid you welcome.
A pyramid of light you seem,
  A galaxy of stars that gleam.
[Repeat first two lines.]

Oh Christmas Tree, Oh Christmas Tree,
  You fill the air with fragrance.
You shrink to very tiny size,
  Reflected in the children's eyes.
[Repeat first two lines.]

Oh Christmas Tree, Oh Christmas Tree,
  What presents do you shelter?

Rich wrappings hide the gifts from sight,
  Done up in bows and ribbons tight.
[Repeat first two lines.]

Oh Christmas Tree, Oh Christmas Tree,
  Your green limbs teach a lesson:
That constancy and faithful cheer
  Are gifts to cherish all the year.
[Repeat first two lines.]

JOLLY OLD SAINT NICHOLAS

Jolly old Saint Nicholas,
    Lean your ear this way.
Don't you tell a single soul
    What I'm going to say.
Christmas Eve is coming soon!
    Now, you dear old man,
Whisper what you'll bring to me.
    Tell me, if you can.

When the clock is striking twelve,
    When I'm fast asleep,
Down the chimney broad and black
    With your pack you'll creep.
All the stockings you will find,
    Hanging in a row.
Mine will be the shortest one—
    You'll be sure to know.

Johnny wants a pair of skates.
    Mary wants a sled.
Susie wants a picture book—
    One she's never read.
Now I think I'll leave to you
    What to give the rest.
Choose for me, dear Santa Claus—
    You will know the best.

OH HOLY NIGHT!

Oh holy night! The stars are brightly shining.
It is the night of the dear Savior's birth.
Long lay the world in sin and error pining,
   Till He appeared, and the soul felt its worth.
A thrill of hope the weary world rejoices,
   For yonder breaks a new and glorious morn.
Fall on your knees!
   Oh, hear the angel voices!
   Oh night divine! Oh night when Christ was born!
   Oh night divine! Oh night, oh night divine!

Drawn by the light of Faith serenely beaming,
   With glowing hearts, by His cradle we stand.
So, led by one bright star so sweetly beaming,
   Here came three Wise Men from Orient land.
The King of Kings lay thus in humble manger,
   In all our trials born to be our friend.
He knows our need;
   To our weakness no stranger!
   Behold your King! Before the Infant bend!
   Behold your King, your King! Before Him bend!

Truly He taught us to love one another.
   His law is love, and His gospel is peace.
Chains shall He break, for the slave is our brother,
   And in His name, all oppression shall cease.
Sweet hymns of joy in grateful chorus raise we.
   Let all within us praise His holy name!
Christ is the Lord!

35

[continued]

Then ever, ever praise we,
His pow'r and glory evermore proclaim,
His pow'r and glory forever more!

Midnight is come—oh, hour of deepest mystery!—
    When God Himself chose to live among men
And wrest aside the prison gates of history
    And let mankind into Heaven again.
A slumb'ring Earth awakes to shouts of gladness,
    Redeemed by love, no more in death to lie.
Christians, rejoice!
    And dry your tears of sadness!
    Noel! Noel! Oh, give thanks to God most high!
    Give thanks, give thanks to God most high!

JOY TO THE WORLD

Joy to the world! The Lord is come.
Let Earth receive her King.
Let ev'ry heart prepare Him room,
   And Heav'n and Nature sing,
   And Heav'n and Nature sing,
   And Heav'n, and Heav'n and Nature sing.

Joy to the world! The Savior reigns.
   Let men their songs employ,
While fields and floods, rocks, hills, and plains
   Repeat the sounding joy,
   Repeat the sounding joy,
   Repeat, repeat the sounding joy.

No more let sins and sorrows grow,
   Nor thorns infest the ground.
He comes to make His blessings flow
   Far as the curse is found,
   Far as the curse is found,
   Far as, far as the curse is found.

He rules the world with truth and grace
   And makes the nations prove
The glories of His righteousness
   And wonders of His love,
   And wonders of His love,
   And wonders, wonders of His love.

Oh Come, All Ye Faithful

Oh come, all ye faithful,
  Joyful and triumphant,
Oh come ye, oh come ye to Bethlehem.
  Come and behold Him, born the King of Angels.

CHORUS:
  Oh come, let us adore Him,
  Oh come, let us adore Him,
  Oh come, let us adore Him,
  Christ the Lord!

Sing, choirs of angels,
  Sing in exultation.
Oh Sing, all ye citizens of Heav'n above:
  "Glory to God, glory in the highest."

CHORUS

Oh True God of True God,
  Light of Light eternal,
Lo! He abhors not the Virgin's womb.
  Son of the Father, begotten not created.

CHORUS

Yea, Lord, we greet Thee,
  Born this happy morning.
Jesus, to Thee all glory be giv'n,
  Word of the Father, now in flesh appearing.

CHORUS

We Wish You a Merry Christmas

We wish you a Merry Christmas,
We wish you a Merry Christmas,
We wish you a Merry Christmas
And a Happy New Year!

CHORUS:
Glad tidings we bring
To you and your kin.
We wish you a Merry Christmas,
And a Happy New Year.

The North Wind is blowing colder,
The North Wind is blowing colder,
The North Wind is blowing colder
Than it would appear!

CHORUS

Oh, bring us some figgy pudding,
Oh, bring us some figgy pudding,
Oh, bring us some figgy pudding
And a glass of good cheer!

CHORUS

We won't go until we get some,
We won't go until we get some,
We won't go until we get some
So bring it right here!

CHORUS

We'll sing you some happy carols,
   We'll sing you some happy carols,
We'll sing you some happy carols
   To ravish your ear!

CHORUS

We have quite the finest voices,
   We have quite the finest voices,
We have quite the finest voices
   That you'll ever hear!

CHORUS

We wish you a Merry Christmas,
   We wish you a Merry Christmas,
We wish you a Merry Christmas
   And a Happy New Year!

CHORUS

Oh Little Town of Bethlehem

Oh little town of Bethlehem,
How still we see thee lie!
Above thy deep and dreamless sleep
The silent stars go by.
Yet in thy dark streets shineth
The everlasting light:
The hopes and fears of all the years
Are met in thee tonight.

For Christ is born of Mary,
And gathered all above,
While mortals sleep, the angels keep
Their watch of wond'ring love.
Oh, morning stars together,
Proclaim the holy birth,
And praises sing to God the King,
And peace to men on Earth.

How silently, how silently,
The wondrous gift is giv'n!
So God imparts to human hearts
The blessings of His Heav'n.
No ear may hear His coming,
But in this world of sin,
Where meek souls will receive Him, still
The dear Christ enters in.

Where children pure and happy
Pray to the blessèd Child,

Where misery cries out to Thee,
  Son of the Mother mild;
Where charity stands watching,
  And faith holds wide the door,
The dark night wakes, the glory breaks,
  And Christmas comes once more.

Oh holy Child of Bethlehem,
  Descend to us, we pray.
Cast out our sin and enter in.
  Be born in us today!
We hear the Christmas angels
  Their great glad tidings tell.
Oh, come to us, abide with us,
  Our Lord Emmanuel.

Up on the Rooftop

Up on the rooftop, reindeer pause.
Out jumps good old Santa Claus!
Down through the chimney, with lots of toys—
  All for the little ones' Christmas joys.

CHORUS:
Ho, ho, ho! Who wouldn't go?
Ho, ho, ho! Who wouldn't go
Up on the rooftop—Click, click, click!—
Down through the chimney with good St. Nick?

First comes the stocking of little Nell.
  Oh, dear Santa, fill it well!
Give her a dolly that laughs and cries,
  One that can open and shut her eyes.

CHORUS

Next hangs the stocking of brother Will.
  It won't take very much to fill—
Give him a hammer and lots of tacks,
  Plus a red ball and a whip that cracks.

CHORUS

Reindeer are restless beside your sleigh,
  Eager to leave and be on their way.
But on the mantel, I've left for you
  Apples, an orange, and warm milk too.

CHORUS

Last is a stocking that's deep and strong—
    I've been a good boy all year long!
Please, if you have them, and if they'll fit,
    Give me a bat and a catcher's mitt.

CHORUS

WHAT CHILD IS THIS?

What Child is this who, laid to rest,
On Mary's lap is sleeping;
Whom angels greet with anthems sweet,
    While shepherds watch are keeping?

CHORUS:
    This, this is Christ the King,
    Whom shepherds guard and angels sing.
    Haste, haste to bring Him laud,
    The Babe, the Son of Mary.

Why lies He in such mean estate,
    Where ox and ass are feeding?
Good Christian, fear for sinners here,
    The silent Word is pleading.

CHORUS

So bring Him incense, gold, and myrrh.
    Come, peasants, kings, to own Him.
The King of Kings salvation brings—
    Let loving hearts enthrone Him!

CHORUS

The old year now away is fled,
    The New Year now is enterèd.
Then let us now our sins downtread,
    And joyfully all appear.

New Chorus:
Merry be the holiday,
And let us run with sport and play.
Hang sorrow, cast care away.
God send you a Happy New Year!

And now, best wishes all good friends
    Unto each other they do send.
Oh, grant we may our lives amend,
    And have no one's blame to fear.

New Chorus

Like the snake, cast off your skin
    Of evil thoughts and wicked sin.
To better this New Year begin.
    God send us a Happy New Year!

New Chorus

SILENT NIGHT

Silent night, holy night!
All is calm, all is bright
'Round yon Virgin Mother and Child—
    Holy infant, so tender and mild.
Sleep in heavenly peace,
Sleep in heavenly peace.

Silent night, holy night!
    Shepherds quake at the sight.
Glories stream from Heaven afar,
    Heav'nly hosts sing "Alleluia,
Christ the Savior is born,
Christ the Savior is born!"

Silent night, holy night!
    Son of God, love's pure light,
Radiance beams from Thy holy face,
    With the dawn of redeeming grace.
Jesus, Lord at Thy birth,
Jesus, Lord at Thy birth!